How To Catch A Cybersquatter
By: Dale D. McGinnis

Consultant of GANUS Law Office
Ddm408@gmail.com;
dmcginni@poets.whittier.edu
Los Angeles, California
323.336.1693

Introduction

If you arrived at this article via a keyword or link confusingly similar to the show *To Catch A Predator[1]*,

1

allow me to quickly dispel any confusion by diverting your attention to the real topic- Cybersquatters. Anyone with an online presence has a cell phone, tablet, or personal computer. The point being that the domineering Internet is at anyone's fingertips[2]. The Internet is used for a broad spectrum of reasons. Like a colorful rainbow, citizens from all over the world walk the inter-web using this powerful tool that has, in less than three decades, changed the paradigm of our global economy. It easily follows, certain powerful and

---

[1] "Ethics of NBC's Sting Show 'To Catch a Predator'", Talk of the Nation, National Public Radio, January 16, 2007; "The Shame Game", Columbia Journalism Review, January–February 2007. Retrieved March 12, 2008.
[2] "The internet at Your Fingertips" by Michael Miller- cyber-master's tips at one's fingertips; How the web went world wide, Mark Ward, Technology Correspondent, BBC News; "World Internet Users and Population Stats". *Internet World Stats*. Miniwatts Marketing Group. 22 June 2011.

unavoidable characteristics of human nature bleed into this cyber world. For the sake of time, let us focus on the most powerful motivator-money. Make no mistake, money is important. Without money, most societies would be unable to develop, and integrate themselves into the global economy[3]. But, money is only a tool used to embellish the monetary value of commodities. And with the Internet, access to the Global consumers' wallet is a lot easier than the old door-to-door sales. It easily follows; commercial enterprises from all over the world now wish to take a piece of the cyber-world-cake.

If we have learned anything from shows like Mad Men[4] or social

---

[3] Mankiw, N. Gregory (2007). "2". *Macroeconomics* (6th ed.). New York: Worth Publishers
[4] Witchel, Alex (June 22, 2008). "'Mad Men' Has Its Moment". *The*

platforms like Facebook[5], it is that advertising pays. And for the most part, advertising has progressed along with the exploration of the inter-web. And instead of witty TV ads, radio jingles, and billboard campaigns, advertisement is done with the help of certain domain names. The domain name directs online traffic towards that particular web page, and from there, other links with advertisements are posted. Google pays-per-click[6]. Anyone can register a domain name, and hold that name, until the registration period

New York Times (The New York Times Company). Retrieved July 5, 2008.

[5] Eldon, Eric (December 18, 2008). "2008 Growth Puts Facebook In Better Position to Make Money". *VentureBeat* (San Francisco). Retrieved December 19, 2008. Also named after a famous colloquialism for the dictionary.

[6] Vise, David A. (October 21, 2005). "Online Ads Give Google Huge Gain in Profit". *The Washington Post*.

laps, and it is relatively cheap. And, there in lies the problem.

Cybersquatting is a rush. But it is important not to rush, when identifying one. For instance, aside from a commercial enterprise, an individual may want to create a domain registrar in order to do what is called 'domaining'. These 'domaineers' registrar a series of domain names, and later develop the web sites for the same reason the commercial enterprises do-advertising. But, it is when domaineers or individuals cross this grey area, and register certain domain names that are associated with famous personalities like Kevin Spacey[7] or Madonna[8] or with

---

[7] Kevin Spacey v. Alberta Hot Rods (NAF Decision - August 1, 2002)
[8] *See Madonna Ciccone, p/k/a Madonna v. Dan Parisi and*

trademarks like SafeGuard[9] and IKEA[10]. Leading them to ensue a domain name dispute. Furthermore with programs and tools used to secure privacy, identifying and catching a Cybersquatter can be next to impossible. Therefore, for the purpose of this article, I will layout a strategic guide to identify a Cybersquatter and reclaim a domain name.

History

The Bureaux Internationaux Reunis pour la Protection de la Propiete Intellectuelle (BIRPI), now

---

'Madonna.com', WIPO Case No. D2000-0847.

[9] The Procter & Gamble Company v. Shanghai Chenxuan Intelligence Technology Development Co. Ltd, People's Republic of China Shanhai Superior People's Court (2001) hu Gao Zhi Zhong Zi no. 4.

[10] Protecting Famous Trademarks in Domain Names, by Jin Ling (Domain Notes - August 17, 2000)

known as The World Intellectual Property Organization (WIPO), established The Paris Convention for the Protection of Industrial Property which is an international treaty establishing a reciprocal protection of intellectual property rights to all its members, known as a priority right. It was signed in Paris, France, on 20 March 1883, and allows trademarks and patents in other countries to use his or her registration of his or her marks a 'first-filing' in other countries apart of the union, and it is still in affect as of today.

The Internet Corporation for Assigned Numbers and Names (ICANN) is a nonprofit organization founded in 1998 that handles the global domain name system, which uses the Uniform Domain Name

Dispute Resolution Policy (UDRP) and rules. After the enactment of The Anticybersquatting Consumer Protect Act (ACPA), the ICANN, through the WIPO, created a report, known as the WIPO report, which established three steps to handle abusive registration of domain names or cybersquatters.

The China Internet Network Information Center (CNNIC) is the administrative agency that handles the domain name system in China, and it established its Domain Name Dispute Resolution Policy (DNDRP) and rules in 2002 and amended them again in 2006. Whether the domain name was registered with ICANN or the CNNIC, domain name disputes can be heard in various Arbitration bodies validated by these systems, or they may end up in civil or federal court [11]. For the sake of time, the following guide will focus on the ICANN's UDRP and rules and CNNIC's DNDRP and rules, and the steps that each panel will consider when identifying a Cybersquatter. The following procedure, complaint, ceases and desist letter, and remedy will adhere to ICANN'S UDRP and rules and WIPO case law, but will sight CNNIC'S DNDRP and rules for purposes of reference.

1. Procedure

Any person can file a claim with a Domain Name Dispute Resolution Institution if a domain name conflicts with his or her intellectual property

---

[11] CNNIC'S DNDRP and Rules Article 15

rights[12]. Depending on where the domain name was registered, a certain institution will hear a dispute[13]. However, certain institutions, like the CNNIC, have a statute of limitation of two years after the domain name was registered[14]. The language accepted by the institution also depends on where the domain name was registered, and under special circumstances may change; however, the institution ultimately decides which language to use[15].

Each party must submit all relevant documents to 1) the other party, 2) the panel of experts, and 3) the institution[16]. The documents are sent via the contact information

---

[12] Id. at Article 2
[13] Id.
[14] Id.
[15] Id. at Article 6
[16] Id. at Article 4

registered in the WHIPO database[17]. The documents may be sent via post mail, facsimile, address, in an electronic form via email, or any other contact information made available in the database[18]. The complainant must make a successful claim containing the following three elements: 1) the respondent's domain name is identical or confusingly similar to his or her trademark, 2) the respondent has no right or legitimate interest in the domain name, and 3) the respondent has registered and used the domain name in bad faith[19].

The complaint and response are limited to 5,000 words[20]. If the institution finds that the complaint is

---

[17] Id.
[18] Id.
[19] Id. at Article 7; ICANN'S UDRP and Rules 4(c)
[20] UDRP Id. at Rule 10

deficient, the complainant has five calendar days to correct and send the amended complaint[21]. Failure of the complainant to identify the domain holder may result in a claim against the registrar or simply a failure of the respondent to file a response[22]. The respondent has 20 calendar days from the initial complaint filed to respond[23]. Failure to respond leaves the panel to determine the case based on the facts and evidence provided by the complainant, including reasonable inferences made[24].

The complainant and the respondent bare the burden of providing evidence and establishing his or her claim[25]. Likewise, they

[21] Id. at Article 14
[22] Id. at Article 31
[23] Id. at Article 17
[24] Id. at Article 31
[25] Id. at Article 7

may choose a panel of the following: 1) a single panelist, 2) a panel of three, lead by a chief panelist, or 3) elect the institution to choose for them[26]. The complainant bares the cost of the institution in most cases, which must be paid within 8 calendar days of the institution receiving the complaint[27]. In some jurisdictions, like areas of China, the institution allows for a dispute to be filed with the local court before or during the proceedings with the institution[28]. The institution decides whether to accept an appeal based on the facts and circumstances[29]. Otherwise, the panel's decision will not be effective over that decision, unless after 10

---

[26] Id. at Article 5
[27] Id. at Article 47
[28] Id. at Article 15
[29] ICANN's UDRP and rules paragraph 10

days after the award, a complaint is not made or the court denies the hearing[30].

2. Complaint

As an ICANN DRPR panelist with over 150 reported decisions, Mark V. B. Partridge gives six recommendations when filing a complaint or response, "1) the complaint or answer should be brief, 2) the pleadings should be brief, 3) the pleadings should follow the UDRP or appropriate policy and rules depending on jurisdiction, 4) support each element or position with proof, 5) make good use of supporting authority, and 6) recognize the limits of the UDRP or

---

[30] Id. at Article 16, 17

appropriate policy and rules depending on jurisdiction"[31]. A decision from the panel ends with the application of the policy to the record presented in the dispute, which is: to curb the abusive registration of domain names in circumstances where the registrant is seeking to profit from and exploit the trademark of another.

A. Identical or Confusingly Similar

It is difficult to determine each institution's jurisdictional approach, however, ICANN'S UDRP and rules state that the panel evaluates solely on comparison of the complainant's

---

[31] Mark V. B., Patridge. "Options." *Alternative Dispute Resolution An Essential Competency for Lawyers.* NEW YORK: OXFORD, 2009. 32-69. Print.

mark and the alphanumeric string constituting the domain name. However, the complainant must establish rights in his or her trademark first.

1. Rights

In order for a complainant to establish rights in his or her trademark, they must provide 1) date of trademark registration or 2) common law rights. The date of a trademark registration can be provided from simply asking the trademark office, where it was registered, to provide a copy of registration. However, providing proof of common law rights varies depending on national jurisdiction. According to an overview of WIPO panels on selected UDRP decisions, a complainant must show that the mark has become a distinctive identifier associated with the complainant or its goods or services[32]. Evidence of such includes: length and amount of sales under the mark, the nature and extent of advertising, and consumer surveys, and media recognition[33]. Personal names are only protectable if used commercially to establish trademark rights. Thus, celebrities such as Madonna, Julia Roberts, Spike Lee, Freddy Abu, and Kevin Spacey have obtained relief under the UDRP[34].

2. Identical or Confusingly Similar

---

[32] bet365 Group Limited v. Domains by Proxy, Inc. / Steve Prime (38,39,40); WIPO 2.0

[33] Id. at 40

[34] Mark V. B., Patridge. "Options." *Alternative Dispute Resolution An Essential Competency for Lawyers.* NEW YORK: OXFORD, 2009. 32-69. Print.

Once the complainant has established a right in his or her trademark, the panel compares the mark and the domain name along, independent of the use factors usually considered in a traditional trademark infringement action[35]. Considering the trademark is 'well-known' and highly recognizable, a domain name that incorporates the entire trademark[36], contains the addition of generic or descriptive terms[37], additional common words[38],

---

[35] See *Banconsumer Service, Inc. v. Mary Langthorne, Financial Advisor,* <u>WIPO Case No. D2001-1367</u>; *InfoSpace.com, Inc. v. Delighters, Inc. d/b/a Cyber Joe's Internet Cafe,* <u>WIPO Case No. D2000-0068.</u>

[36] See, *e.g., Telstra Corporation v. Barry Cheng Kwok Chu,* WIPO Case No. D2000-0423; *Pfizer Inc. v. United Pharmacy Ltd,* WIPO Case No. D2001-0446; *E.I. du Pont de Nemours and Company v. Richi Industry S. r. l.,* WIPO Case No. D2001-1206; *Utensilerie Associate S. p. A. v. C & M,* WIPO Case No. D2003-0159; *Lilly Icos LLC. v. John Hopking/Neo net Ltd.,* WIPO Case No. D2005-0694; *Shaw Industries Group Inc., Columbia Insurance Company v. Wan-Fu China, Ltd.,* WIPO Case No. D2007-0282.

[37] *V&S Vin&Sprit AhB v. Giovanni Pastore,* WIPO Case No. D2002-0926; *Thomson Broadcast and Media Solution Inc., Thomson v.*

additional geographical terms[39], additional generic top-level domain suffixes[40], has spaces between letters[41], or is visually or aurally comparative[42] may be considered identical or confusingly similar.

However, the WIPO overview evaluates confusion on the following factors, which risk that Internet users

---

Alvaro Collazo, WIPO Case No. D2004-0746; *Sanofi-Aventis v. US-Meds.com*, WIPO Case No. D2004-0809; and *F. Hoffman La Roche AG v.Pinetree Development, Ltd.*, WIPO Case No. D2006-0049.

[38] See, *e.g.*, *Hoffmann-La Roche Inc. v. Hightech Industries, Andrew Browne*, WIPO Case No. D2010-0240; *Wal-Mart Stores, Inc. v. Richard MacLeod d/b/a For Sale*, WIPO Case No. D2000-0662.

[39] F. Hoffmann-LA Roche AG v. Whoisguard Protected/ Sallu Org, Salman Baig, (3), WIPO Case No. D2014-0480.

[40] *RX America, LLC v. Mattew Smith*, WIPO Case No. D2005-0540; *Sanofi-Aventis v. US Online Pharmacies*, WIPO Case No. D2006-0582.

[41] See, *Wembley Nat'l Stadium Ltd. v. Thomson*, WIPO Case No. D2000-1233 (November 16, 2000) (domain name www.wembleystadium.net identical to "WEMBLEY STADIUM" mark; transfer ordered);*Julie & Jason, Inc. d/b/a The Mah Jongg Maven v. Faye Scher d/b/a Where the Winds Blow*, WIPO Case No. D2005-0073 (March 6, 2005)

[42] Alrosa v. Domain Privacy LTD, DNS Admin / The Tidewinds Group, Inc. and Elisa Marina Mendoza Rosa, (28), WIPO Case No. D2013-0256

may actually believe there to be a real connection between the domain name and the complaint and or its goods and services: 1) overall impression created by the domain name, 2) the distinguishing value of any terms, 3) the letters or number in the domain name additional to the relied-upon mark, and 4) whether an Internet user unfamiliar with any meaning of the disputed domain name seeking the complaint's goods or services on the worldwide web would necessarily comprehend such distinguishing value vi-a-vi the relevant mark[43]. And in the assessment of this risk, the content of a website would usually be disregarded[44].

---

[43] bet365 Group Limited v. Domains by Proxy, Inc. / Steve Prime ,(34,39), WIPO Case No. D2011-1241.
[44] Id. at 40

B. Right or Legitimate Interests

After the complainant has made an initial prima facie case, establishing his or her trademark rights and similarity, the respondent carries the burden of demonstrating his or her right or legitimate interest in the domain name[45]. If the respondent fails, the complaint has succeeded[46]. The respondent may establish by demonstrating: before any notice to it of the dispute, the use of, or demonstrable preparation to use, the domain name or a name

---

[45] 4(a)(ii) of the UDRP. WIPO Overview 2.0, paragraph 2.1; *Croatia Airlines d.d. v. Modern Empire Internet Ltd.*, WIPO Case No. D2003 0455; *Belupo d.d. v. WACHEM d.o.o.*, WIPO Case No. D2004-0110; *MetAmerica Mortgage Bankers v. Whois ID Theft Protection c/o Domain Admin*, NAF Claim No. FA0611000852581
[46] paragraph 4(a)(ii) of the UDRP

corresponding to the domain name is connected with a bona fide offering of goods or service[47], 2) they have been commonly known by the domain name, even if it has acquired no trademark or service mark rights[48], and 3) they are making a legitimate noncommercial or fair use of the domain name, without intent for commercial gain to misleadingly divert consumers or to tarnish the trademark or service mark at issue[49].

1. Before notice, bona fide offering of goods or services

The respondent must have used his or her domain name for a service or good before the complainant notified the respondent of the

---

[47] paragraph 4(c) of the Policy
[48] Id.
[49] Id.

trademark, name, or goods and services offered[50]. However, if the complainant contacts the respondent giving notice of infringement, such as a cease and desist, and the respondent does not respond, does not contests rights, or hides his or her identity, an inference that the respondent did not have rights and knew of the complainant's rights can be made, and because the respondent failed to respond, no plausible reason for registering the domain name other than for the association with the complainant's trademark can be made[51]. However if the respondent identifies that they have used his or her domain name, before notice, for

---

[50] ICANN'S UDRP and rules paragraph 4(a)(ii)

[51] Detur International B.V., Tatil Sevahat Turm Anonim Sirketi v. Bertical Axis Inc., WIPO Case No. D2012-0919.

bona fide goods or services, they will have satisfied this element[52].

2. Commonly known by the domain name

In special circumstances, a domain name holder may have registered her domain name based on her name or nickname[53], or because of a common dictionary name of which they thought to associate with the domain name[54]. Otherwise, the respondent must provide a plausible explanation between the complainant's trademark and his or her domain name[55], like in Sting v.

---

[52] See Gordon Summer p/k/a Sting v. Michael Urvan, Case No. 2000-0596 (WIPO July 24, 2000).

[53] Alrosa v. Domain Privacy LTD, DNS Admin / The Tidewinds Group, Inc. and Elisa Marina Mendoza Rosa, WIPO Case No. D2013-0256

[54] See *Mobile Communication Service Inc. v. WebReg, RN*, WIPO Case No. D2005-1304.

[55] *See Madonna Ciccone, p/k/a Madonna v. Dan Parisi and 'Madonna.com'*, WIPO Case No. D2000-0847.

Michael Urvan where there was
evidence that the Respondent had
made bona fide use of the name Sting
prior to obtaining the domain name
registration and there was no
indication that he was seeking to
trade on the goodwill of the well-
known singer[56].

3. Noncommercial or fair use, without intent of commercial gain

The respondent must prove that
the domain name was registered for
the purpose of noncommercial or fair
use. As was discussed above, any
evidence of commercial uses or
profit can be used against the
respondent. If the respondent uses his

---

[56] See Gordon Summer p/k/a Sting v. Michael Urvan, Case No.
2000-0596 (WIPO July 24, 2000).

or her domain name for the following: offering sponsored links[57], pay-per-click parking page deriving revenue[58], a directory of commercial websites[59], provide links to other sites being competitors of the Complainant, and of an apparently commercial nature from which the respondent intends to derive profit from the association of the complainant's mark[60] they will have used the domain name for a noncommercial or for commercial gain.

---

[57] See *Mudd, LLC v. Unasi, Inc.*, WIPO Case No. D2005-0591; and *Volvo Trademark Holding AB v. Unais, Inc.*, WIPO Case No. D2005-0556.

[58] paragraph 4(b)(iv) of the Policy (see *Villeroy & Boch AG v. Mario Pingerna* WIPO Case No. D2007-1912).

[59] *Asian World of Martial Arts Inc. v. Texas International Property Associates*, WIPO Case No. D2007-1415 and *Bayerische Motoren Werke AG v. (This Domain is For Sale) Joshuathan Investments, Inc.*, WIPO Case No. D2002-0787

[60] See also *inter alia Sports Holdings, Inc. v. Whois ID Theft Protection*, WIPO Case No. D2006-1146

C. Bad Faith Registration and Use

The respondent must have a purpose for registering and selecting a particular domain name[61]. That purpose must not be to intentionally attract, for commercial gain, the Internet users to his or her Web site or other online location, by creating a likelihood of confusion with the Complainant's mark as to the source, sponsorship, affiliation, or endorsement of his or her Web site or location or of a product or service on his or her Web site Location[62]. The

---

[61] Sanofi v. Farris Nawas, (3), WIPO Case No. D2014-0705

respondent is responsible for the content of the website[63]. The panel determines the respondent's intent by balancing the probabilities[64]. These probabilities are not exhaustive[65] and may be the following: offering the domain name for sale[66], passive holding[67], not responding to the complaint or behavior associated with cyberflying[68], lack of any plausible legitimate use[69], identical or confusingly similar names, lack of

---

[62] See *inter alia, Manheim Auctions Inc. v. Whois ID Theft Protection*, WIPO Case No. D2006-1044; Fry's *Electronics, Inc v. Whois ID Theft Protection*, WIPO Case No. D2006-1435; Barry D. Sears, Ph.D. v. YY / Yi Yanlin WIPO Case No. D2007-0286).

[63] Quester Group, Inc. v. Domain Capital **39**

[64] Total S.A v. Gustavo Cerda, (6), WIPO Case No. D2011-2073.

[65] See *Telstra Corporation Limited v. Nuclear Marshmallows*, WIPO Case No. D2000-0003

[66] See, e.g., *Bayerische Motoren Werke AG v. (This **Domain** is For Sale) Joshuathan Investments, Inc.*, WIPO Case No. D2002-0787.

[67] see the landmark case*Telstra Corporation Limited v. Nuclear Marshmallows*, WIPO Case No. D2000-0003

[68] HSBC Finance Corporation v. Clear Blue Sky Inc. and Domain Manager, (42), WIPO Case No. D2007-0062.

[69] *See Madonna Ciccone, p/k/a Madonna v. Dan Parisi and 'Madonna.com'*, WIPO Case No. D2000-0847.

due diligence[70], website activity[71],
pattern of conduct[72], sites linked to
the domain name[73], reverse hijacking[74],
 opportunistic bad faith[75], and
location of a product or service on
the website[76]. The use of a disclaimer
is not sufficient[77].

3. Cease and Desist

---

[70] *inter alia* in *Execujet Holdings Ltd. v. Air Alpha America, Inc,* WIPO Case D2002-0669.

[71] Mission Kwasizabantu, Complainant v. Benjamin Rost, Respondent, (6), WIPO Case No. D2000-0279.

[72] Mercer Human Resource Consulting, Ltd., Mercer Human Resource Consulting Inc. v. Konstantinos Zournas **46** (one is not enough); *Reasearch in Motion Limited v. Pacific Rim System*, WIPO Case No. D2001-0408; *Valeant Pharmaceuticals International and Valeant Canada Limited v. Johnny Carpela*, WIPO Case No. D2005-0786.

[73] Id.

[74] bet365 Group Limited v. Domains by Proxy, Inc. / Steve Prime ,(61), WIPO Case No. D2011-1241.

[75] See *SSL International PLC v. Mark Freeman*, WIPO Case No. D2000-1080; *Perfumes Christian Dior v. Javier Garcia Quintas and Christian Dior. net*, WIPO Case No. D2000-0226; *Veuve Clicquot Ponsardin, Maison Fondée en 1772 v. The Polygenix Group Co.*, WIPO Case No. D2000-0163.

[76] Pancil LLC, Complainant v. Henry Chan, Respondent, (4), WIPO Case No. D2003-1033.

[77] See *Madonna Ciccone, p/k/a Madonna v. Dan Parisi and 'Madonna.com'*, WIPO Case No. D2000-0847.

The cease and desist letter must be sent as soon as the complainant becomes aware of the domain name at issue. If the domain name holder uses the domain name before it is notified for bona fide services or goods or it is notified without the complainant disclosing their rights and identity, then the domain holder may satisfy the second element. If the complainant has no issue with satisfying the first element, identical or confusingly similar and rights and legitimate interest, then the letter is merely a formal requirement because, as discussed above, the burden shifts to the respondent. However, for the complainants who have an issue satisfying this element, it may be very difficult to collect information, which is almost exclusively within the knowledge of the respondent when satisfying the third element of intent. This element represents an opportunity to prove that the domain holder registered and used the domain name in bad faith. Therefore, it is imperative to collect as much evidence as possible to tip the scale when it comes to balancing the probabilities. The panel may accept an email or response to a communication by the respondent as an answer, given the respondent does not file a formal answer, or as evidence of intent[78]. The email, therefore, may be a reliable indicator of the respondent's intentions, and even more for when the respondent does not respond to the

---

[78] Sanofi v. Farris Nawas, (3), <u>WIPO Case No. D2014-0705</u>

complainant's contentions set out in the complaint[79]. The following is advise, and in no way encapsulates a full proof plan for obtaining information through communication, considering each case is unique deepening on the circumstances.

If the domain holder does no respond to the complaint or does not respond to the cease and desist letter, it merely assist the complainant because a likely inference will be that the domain holder does not attest to the facts and evidence before the panel or the rights being asserted by the complainant. Therefore, any attempt to communicate with the respondent can be helpful. And if the complainant can open a channel of communication, and ploy certain

---

[79] Id. at 4

techniques- the cybersquatter may disclose information willingly. Any communication with the cybersquatter may be the only opportunity to resolve the domain name dispute.

First, the domain name and web site's activity should be monitored at all times. The activity from this web site and its links may provide the evidence necessary to prove that it is being used for noncommercial uses whether it is by diverting traffic for pay clicking or tarnishing the trademark. Before the complainant unveils its identity, it may choose to initially communicate under an alias. Any threating presence may ward the cybersquatter away. The alias can assist the complainant to ask for an offer from the cybersquatter, which may disclose the evidence needed. The complainant must maintain the alias. The idea is to provide evidence of bad faith registration and use through selling the domain name for an inflated price, which is also evidence of registering the site for a non-commercial purpose. The complainant must ask, because the cybersquatter cannot be compelled to sell and the price must come from the respondent. The intent, which is knowledge, purpose, or desire, must come from the cybersquatter.

Secondly, the first attempt at communication, without an alias, must notify the cybersquatter or respondent of the right and legitimate interest the complainant has in the domain name, ask the cybersquatter or respondent to cease and desist his or her activity, and ask for them to transfer or 'offer' a price for purchase. Again, this first attempt at communication should be strongly worded insisting that the domain name holder has no rights, stating the complainant case clearly and persuasively, and then emphasizing that the complainant is willing to purchase the domain name at a price offered by the domain name holder. The information acquired from the first attempt at communication will help the complainant assess the cybersquatter's true motive or intent. With the fear of legal circumstances, the Cybersquatter may react to the pressure.

Thirdly, the first attempt at communication may be the last. Therefore, the complainant must make sure to end the communication with an offer to settle. If at the very least, the idea is to save the complainant the most amount of money. Considering that the domain name can open up tremendous amounts of revenue, and that revenue is based on the amount of time it takes to resolve the dispute- every second counts. If the domain name holder fails to respond, then the complainant must move forward with his or her complaint and continue to send communications reiterating his or her case, and attempting to settle without dissolving the complainant persuasive case. If all else fails, any response from the domain name holder can be used and given to the panel when balancing the possibilities for bad faith. In any sense the following proponents should be included in the communication between the complainant and the respondent: notice of infringement of trademark, request to disclose identity or contract information, request to stop using trademarks, set a deadline for response, further suggest lack of rights or legitimate interest in the domain name, list accurate contract information, send a physical letter to the address(s) listed on the registrar, notice of denial of infringement or not, whether the respondent defects liability or not, extend the deadline if need be to allow respondent time to comply with the demands set forth, and retain valid copies for the Panel. This list in not exhaustive, and meanwhile, the website should be followed closely in order to keep track of the respondent's activities. If enough detail and attention is put into this letter, it can affectively save the clients time and money in resolving the domain dispute possibly before it even starts. If the case does end in an administrative hearing or civil court, the client needs to know the cost.

4. Remedy

A client must understand the costs for bringing a Domain Name Dispute for each situation and circumstance. For instance, a dispute in civil court involves costly litigation, DNDRC is cheaper, paying the cyber-squatter's nuisance value may be cheaper, and registering the domain name before someone else is the cheapest alternative, if applicable. Keeping in mind, the longer the domain dispute lasts, the larger the losses the trademark owner will suffer, considering they are a commercial enterprise and his or her site brings in low to high revenue.

5. Conclusion

In conclusion, a trademark owner's claim is only as strong as the evidence they provide showing his or her trademark is commonly known among the general public at the time of registration of the domain name in dispute[80] in the particular geographical location. However in some cases, a panel might infer from

---

[80] Mercer Human Resource Consulting, LTD., Mercer Human Resource Consulting Inc., Complainant v. Konstantinos Zournas, Respondent, (16), WIPO Case No. D2007-1425.

evidence that a respondent was not aware of a particular trademark when registering the domain name[81]. A panel decides how 'well-known' a trademark is in a particular geographical area depending on the category of the famous name, such as Coca-Cola being very famous[82], which proof of advertising may avail. Therefore, aside from folding and purchase the domain name from the cybersquatter, the best idea is to closely monitor the cybersquatters past and present activity, and attempt at opening a channel of communication to disclose evidence or reach a settlement before too much time and money is lost because evidence of the respondent's

---

[81] Id. at 17
[82] Id.

awareness of a particular trademark is the key to catching a cybersquatter[83].

---

[83] Id.

www.ingramcontent.com/pod-product-compliance
Lightning Source LLC
Chambersburg PA
CBHW030738180526
45157CB00008BA/3218